Little Budgie's Done A Fudgie

By
Simon Harris

Little Budgie's done a fudgie.
He shouts, 'Mummy! Nappy!'
So Mummy Budgie says to him,
'Hey listen, cheeky chappy!'

'The next time that you need a poo,
just shout 'Hey Mummy, quick!'
'As I have something big boys use.'
'A potty does the trick!'

Little Budgie's done a fudgie.
He shouts, 'Oh no! Mummy!'
'I really tried so very hard.'
'But it hurt my tummy.'

Mummy Budgie says, 'Don't worry!'
'Hey you tried your best.'
'I'll clean you up. You'll try again.'
'You'll pass the potty test!'

Little Budgie's done a fudgie.
He got oh so near!
So Mummy Budgie says, 'There, there.'
'You almost made it dear.'

'Don't give up son. I'll tell you what.'
'How about a nice treat?'
'Just make it there. Sit down in time.'
'You'll get a prize to eat!'

Little Budgie's with his toys,
and he feels down below.

He jumps and runs, fast as he can!
He knows it's time to go.

Little Budgie's done a fudgie.
He made it. Clever boy!
Mummy Budgie says, 'Well done son!'
She flaps and jumps for joy!

She looks inside, the potty's full,
as he has pooed and weed.

She takes him off, into the town,
and buys him special seed.

Little Budgie did a fudgie.
His nappy days are done.
The wees and poos, day time and night.
This potty stuff is fun!

When this birdie thinks he's ready,
he'll move on to the loo.
So just remember little one.
If he can, you can too!

The End

Printed in Great Britain
by Amazon